THE TRAVELS OF A
SERVICE DOG
STORIES OF SCOTTY

THE TRAVELS OF A
SERVICE DOG

STORIES OF SCOTTY

ANA E. RIVERA-CASTILLO

CITI OF
BOOKS

CITIOFBOOKS, INC.
3736 Eubank NE Suite A1
Albuquerque, NM 87111-3579
www.citiofbooks.com
Hotline: 1 (877) 389-2759
Fax: 1 (505) 930-7244

Ordering Information:
Quantity sales. Special discounts are available on quantity purchases by corporations, associations, and others. For details, contact the publisher at the address above.

Printed in the United States of America.

ISBN-13:   Softcover   979-8-89391-941-7
            eBook   979-8-89391-943-1
            Hardback   979-8-89391-942-4

Library of Congress Control Number:

TABLE OF CONTENTS

INTRODUCTION

Ana Elena Rivera is a biologist with a degree from Georgia State University; her hobbies are photography and exploring nature.

Because Ana's mother, Ana Castillo de Rivera, was disable she had to use oxygen and rely on a service dog. A young two-month-old Westy, who she named Scotty, immediately showed all the faculties to be trained as a service dog. He had his service registration and the title of a good citizen only a year later and was busy working with Mrs. Ana Castillo de Rivera, as her faithful companion.

To help him with his training, Scotty traveled to various locations in South Florida along with his classmate, Bellini. When Mrs. Rivera passed away, Scotty was retrained to help his new patient , her daughter, Ana. To recover from the grief at the loss of her mother , Ana decided to travel to The National Parks and other places famous for archaeology and natural phenomena with Scotty, her service dog at her side to seek inner peace and return to a happy life.

Over the last two years, Ana told her niece about her travels with Scotty – from Scotty's viewpoint. Her friends and family convinced Ana to draft the stories so others could enjoy them too.

In this book, Scotty will narrate his travels to his canine friends, recounting anecdotes, and giving his doggy opinions of the National

Parks of the United States and the Yucatan Peninsula. Through their travels, Ana and Scotty come to find happiness once again.

Scotty and Mitzi

CHAPTER 1

SOUTH FLORIDA

Hi Mitzi! (Mitzi is a large, sweet Dalmatian mix gal.) You know my full name is Scotty West. I was given that name because I was born in Kansas in the western United States. My home is now with my family and in Miami. My favorite beach near home is Dania Beach, specifically in Zachary Taylor Park; you can swim safely in a small bay there. And there is a channel you can jump across, although you must always check for crocodiles, and I do not want to be their meal! these parks are areas where mangroves naturally grow, but you can also find Australian pines that were imported to dry the mangroves.

Morningside Park

What is your favorite park in Miami? I imagine it is Morningside. There, you can walk on the trails between the mangroves and cool off in the bay waters.

1

Sometimes, as Bellini (my childhood friend) says we should stay out of the water just in case we run into a crocodile!

I am getting hot, so I am going to rest and enjoy the cool breeze while I tell you all about my trip to the Everglades and its surroundings in South Florida.

The Everglades is a swamp and is full of plants, trees, and different animals. When we went there, we walked the Anhinga Trail. At this National Park we must stay within the tourist centers in this national park because alligators are on the trails and in the water. I saw alligators in the ponds! They are huge!

(9 feet long). Did you know that this is the only place in the world where you can see alligators and crocodiles? You can also see manatees. These animals are very peaceful, they live in the canals and around the bay waters, they are mammals like us.

This area is at the mouth of the river that forms a delta from Lake Chokoloskee, creating a swamp of grasslands.

Everglades

Tree islands or islets are called hammocks, Hammocks are where mangroves, pines, and oaks grow; therefore, animal life, such as deer, black bears, and panthers live here.

The Everglades National Park is so big that there is even a third entrance to the park, Sharky Valley, which is in the center of the marshland. To get to the observation tower, you must get on a tram. The ranger permits you , and then he takes you up in the middle. You can only see something once you reach the base of the tower, and from there, you climb to the top of the central building, where you can see the extensions of the swamp and the islets of trees. Humans can rent a bike or bring one and ride the trail (I do not recommend that because of the big reptiles).

Sharkey Valley

In this national park, the fresh waters mix with those of the sea, finally leaving Lake Chokoloskee slowly and flowing into the Florida bay . Being in the Everglades is a unique experience.

We also drove by through Big Cypress National Park on the way back.

Saw Grass

The Miccosukee Tribe population manages Francis Taylor Wildlife Preserve. You should use great caution while visiting These parks because there are gators everywhere.

While in training, I drove around the Florida peninsula one winter. We first visited a muddy dirt road surrounded by streams and large hammocks. We saw many ducks, herons, anhingas, and gators. The other route is a swampy area surrounded by reeds inhabited by birds, deer, and gators. I wanted to cool off in the swamp, but Ana would not let me. "She told me you're a service dog. You should be calm." How could I be calm? I must be on guard. There are too many gators around, and I must protect her.

I verified that the best time to visit all these parks is in winter, also known as the "dry season." The season goes from the end of November to May because it is not hurricane season. If you go in summer, the bugs will eat you, and you can quickly get dehydrated. It is worth seeing a sunrise in the grasslands, especially at the beginning of the dry season, where you can still see the reflections of the sun's rays in the swamp.

Passing Big Cypress going towards Naples at the Tamiami trail , you will find a detour to the left . That is the way to go to Everglades City and Chokoloskee. Chokoloskee is the last town on the Florida peninsula. It is a typical small southern town with a lovely bay. But here are no beaches. The city of the Everglades is the entrance to the Ten Thousand Islands; it is also the entrance to the Everglades National Park on the west side. I visited there with my friend Bellini, and we both enjoyed the trip. We went boating for ninety minutes at the canals form by the islands and saw the Gulf of Mexico. On the other side of the Florida strait is Yucatan, another peninsula in Mexico. We Learned a lot on this trip ,Mitzi! The guide explained the distinct types of mangroves and how the trees maintain the ecosystem.

Biscayne National Park is in the southeast, at the end of the peninsula. This is one of my favorite parks, because you can see Miami Beach, South Point, and downtown Miami from one vantage point. Sand Key Park is in the ocean and on the coast of the peninsula and has sand banks and keys that you can visit Eliot Key, Boca Chica Key, and Adams Key are the main ones there. We stayed in the peninsula at the visitor center area because we could walk along the trails and safely enter the bay. Biscayne Bay is so peaceful and beautiful, especially in the mornings.

Bill Baggs Cape Florida State Park is in Key Biscayne. The walking and swimming trails are next to the lighthouse, which is a landmark there. Our favorite place is here in Morningside, which I think is your favorite! I visit it whenever I am home. Do you want to go with me one day to the Florida Keys? I have only gone down to Deer Key. But there are many Keys. I have yet to go to Key West. The Florida Keys, or the Conch Republic, as they call themselves, is a 180 kilometers long chain of islands at the end of the Florida peninsula. The Keys is one of the few places in the US where I can watch the sunrise from the sea and the sunset in the same place.

On one occasion, I went to the film festival Humphry Bogart Film Festival with my friend Bellini; There is a famous B&W movie set in Key Largo we also visited Coral Reefs State Park, Harris Beach in Tavernier. Bellini, as always, wanted to avoid getting into the sea and getting its paws full of sand. For me, it is an extraordinary place because it was where I came with Ana's mom for the last time, I remembered her words.

"You must live every moment and enjoy it in a big way, especially with good friends."

****

"That is Scotty. It would be best if you learned to accept things as they are. Tomorrow, tell me about your trip to the southwest."

Scotty at Miami Beach

Scotty talking to Mitzi.

Map of South Florida and the Everglades

CHAPTER 2

US National Parks, Southwest

They say that a naturalist is someone who admires and likes nature.

If so, I am a naturalist! What are you?

Let me tell you about my first trip to the southwestern United States. I was a young boy when Ana, my friend and patient, told me, " Let's Go to the Mountains! Let us go on a road trip. You will see you are going to love it. First, we will go to Las Vegas, but only for one night; the next day, we will go to the Grand Canyon of Colorado on the south rim, and from there, we will travel to Mesa Verde and go around Monument Valley. Then we will rest at Lake Powell. Afterward, we will visit the north rim of the Grand Canyon and return to Las Vegas by Zion National Park.

Honestly, I did not understand what she was saying then. Ana started packing her luggage and a small bag for me. Well, at least my favorite towel, toy, and blankets were in it.

Day 1

Early one morning, she said to me, "Come on! it is time for our trip!" and in forty-five minutes, we were at the airport. I knew what

8

an airport was because this was the place where we usually picked up friends and family when they visited us. What a surprise I got! We went to the counter and then to a small area like a tunnel. I thought we were going to the street. But we entered a long vehicle with three seats on one side and three on the other. We settled into the seats at the end. I felt comfortable lying in my stroller, but suddenly, terror started, and this thing flew into the sky with a horrible noise!

That torment lasted five hours and I was trembling with fear. It was my first flight, and I was terrified. When we landed, I just wanted to run away from there.

We left the airport in the middle of the afternoon, and the heat was dry. I wondered where the grass was as I needed to pee! But there were no trees and not even any grass; it was just sand and cement in this place. I just had to imitate cats.

They say Las Vegas is the city that never sleeps, the city of lights, and I would add noise!

We arrived at a friendly, charming, and smelly cigar hotel called Treasure Island. The noisy area was called the casino.

However, our room was spacious, clean, quiet, and on the eleventh floor. From there, we could see part of the city.

The city was in a valley, and I could see huge hills on the western edge. They are called the mountains. They are part of the Red Rock Canyon.

That night, we had a nice dinner inside the hotel and a tour of its surroundings, where I finally found grass.

Day 2

Everything looks so different compared to our city (Miami). Everywhere here it looks dry, with no trees and lots ofsand. The sand here is compared to that in Miami. This sand is brown and not as salty. (I tasted it.)

Already on the road, we turn off towards a river with a horseshoe-shaped dam called Hoover Dam, considered one of the seven wonders of modern engineering.

The arch-shaped dam is made of concrete, and holds the Colorado River into the Black Canyon, providing electricity to Las Vegas, Henderson, and Southern California.

From the Hoover Dam, we headed east towards Kingman. However, we made a side detour to Highway 66, a famous road from Chicago to California, considered a scenic route.

From there, we headed north to Williams on Highway 64 and noticed that the road began to change. Here, we saw more hills and trees. This area is called the Kaibab National Forest.

We stopped at the village entrance to the park (visitor center). The guides recommended watching a movie in the visitor center for more information and guidance. Wow, it was so real that when the lion showed up in the movie, I could not stand it and growled at it.

Finally, we entered the park. The entrance line was small, and we entered first since we already had a pass. Suddenly, voila, a giant sinkhole! I need to protect Ana from that huge hole! There it was, the Grand Canyon in front of us! The Colorado River was formed more than five million years ago. If I dropped my bone in it, I would not be able to get it back.

We stayed at the Maswik Lodge in the park where we learned that the road to Lake Powell was closed. The guide suggested we stay in Vermillion Canyon or Tuba. Ana decided to see the place's fauna and the Colorado River up close in Vermillion Canyon.

Leaving there, we went to our room. It was in the middle of a forest of pines and firs. It was simple and well-furnished and had all the essentials. Outside was full of animals that I could smell.

That evening, we ended our day with a nice dinner at the prestigious Tovar Hotel on the edge, where we watched the sunset and then had a healthy meal. This was the first hotel in the park. It was built in 1902 and is a historic hotel with different rooms. Dining there requires people to book well in advance; it is already a famous restaurant. When you are there, you can forget about the problems of the city, it is so lovely to enjoy the landscape and the beauty of nature, and that is enough for me. Then, I remembered this saying:

"If you start to see things thoroughly, you may think everything is a mental creation. The reality you see is yours and is the result of your thinking."

That is why, when we are in contact with these wonders, each of us interprets them in our own way and ends up remaining silent.

That night, I kept thinking about everything I had seen in less than twenty-four hours. I was in one of the world's seven natural wonders: I had to be cautious when walking because the Canyon is 123.92 kilometers long, up to twenty-nine kilometers wide, and could be more than 1.6 kilometers deep. It would be difficult to get to the bottom if I dropped something. I also had to keep Ana far from the rim.

The natives of this region have been living here for over one thousand years and have built settlement; they include the Pueblo Nation, the Hualapai Indians, and the Navajo Nation.

Near the Tovar Hotel, you can visit a house of the Anasazi Indians. These natives were very resourceful and built solid mud constructions. They also had hydroponic systems for their crops.

Observing such a wonderful place is impressive, and one can only appreciate that moment and thank our creator.

Day 3

As we wanted to see the sunrise, we got up early and went to the edge of the canyon for breakfast. There are no words to express what I saw: breathtaking views. It was worth seeing.

So, we explored the canyon first, west, and then east, to facilitate Ana to take better pictures because we will have the sun on the back. We were on the south side of the canyon. As you move west, you should stop and take time at all the bus stops to avoid walking so much. It is worth spending time on each visit, especially at Lookout Studio Station, Hopi Point, Monument Creek Vista, and Hermits Rest.

In the afternoon, we went to the east side towards Yaki Point. Here we saw more people. We discover a short trail that leads back to Tovar Hotel, skirting the canyon.

The view was also impressive in this place, but I was too exhausted. So, I asked Ana to take me to the room because I needed a nap. The heat affected me, and the summer temperature can rise to 37.7 degrees Celsius here. I could not take it anymore, and for her to understand me, I refused to take another step and threw myself to the ground.

South Rim

At the lodge, we had dinner at the restaurant. There, we had a view of the forest before the edge. I could appreciate all the different plants and animals that lived around there. I saw deer, squirrels, chipmunks, and moose. The latter was imposing with their moose antlers.

Day 4

We traveled east toward Cameron in the morning and stopped at Desert View Tower. In this place, you can see the Colorado River, and, to the north, the cliffs of the Painted Desert.

We visited the historic Mary Colter Watchtower, where you could have 360-degree tours. Then, we headed towards Highway 64. We were already entering Arizona and Hopi territory, where we observed semi-desert valleys and mountains with different shapes.

Road to Meza Verde

13

We stopped at The Four Corners because it is the only place where four states meet: Colorado, Utah, Arizona, and New Mexico. It is also a Navajo sacred place. On the Colorado Route, we passed monuments like Mexican Hat and Tecc Nous Pos. On our left, we saw the Painted Desert; it is so called because it has different shades of brown, ranging from a reddish brown to a pale yellow. We distinguished from the road the different layers marked years.

As soon as we entered Colorado, we noticed a habitat change. Everything was green, and I saw more semi-desert valleys and hills with plateaus.

After the city of Cortez, we entered a new canyon, and everything was green and full of vegetation.

We began the climb up to 1524 meters. It was a very steep road; at the top, we found the settlement of the Anasazi, ancestors of the Hopi and Nahuatl Indians.

Their houses were built in caves; we had to walk carefully along a path on the edge of an abyss to get there. It was impressive; I saw deer and wild horses. From the hotel, you could see the Rocky Mountains in the distance.

Mesa Verde

Day 5

We decided to take a guided tour to most houses and points of interest, as the road was challenging and steep. Already on the bus, I managed to visualize different landscapes full of trees such as ponderosa pines, juniper, and Douglass firs; there were also native plants (you can see the list on the Meza Verde National Park website).

We visited all the best sites like Badger House, CedarTree Tower, Far View Site, and the Sun Temple. We also saw cliff dwellings, balcony houses, long houses, and spruce houses. However, I did not go to the cliff palace because I could not go down the vertical stairs. They were not made for me, so I watched them from the road with Ana. Either way, I was so tired that I decided to rest.

Day 6

We left the amazing Mesa Verde National Park early the next day and decided to have breakfast in Cortez. Suddenly, we saw four wild goats in the middle of the road.

The original plan was to go from Mesa Verde to Lake Powell. Unfortunately, the roads were closed, so we had to return via route 160 to Tuba and then cross the Colorado River into Marble Canyon; as we returned, we stopped and saw the Monumental Valley. This valley is one of the most beautiful, with rare dry rock formations made by the erosion of the winds. These monuments appear in cowboy movies.

At the intersection of 160 and 89, there is an indigenous village called Tuba; we had lunch in a typical Navajo restaurant. Further on, we crossed the Colorado River in the car and entered Marble Canyon. Elevations vary from 945 meters to 2164 meters. It is located on the Colorado Plateau in northern Arizona,

The hotel was at the canyon's base and has not changed since the early twentieth century. We stayed in a mobile room for the night, so we could appreciate how all these canyons were interconnected. We hoped to see a California condor, but we did not. We could see the Vermillion Cliffs.

Day 7

We left the hotel because we were eager to go to the North Rim of the Grand Canyon. This side is higher than the South Rim. Here, pines and poplars abound. It is colder, and there are more forests and rivers.

We arrived early, so we saw a fantastic view of the lodge, In the back was the view towards the south side of the canyon. The view towards the Southern Rim is more striking.

Impressive!

The hostel we were given was a cabin overlooking the canyon. It was beautiful. Suddenly I saw squirrels. Woof, woof, woof! Let me know if I can catch them! Oh no, I was working, so I controlled myself. Anyway, they escaped me.

During the afternoon, we visited two trails to enjoy the view. If you have the time, they are worth visiting. But if you need more time, stay at the hotel, and enjoy the views. They change by themselves.

Day 8

We left the Grand Canyon early the next day, heading northwest on Kanab Road #89. After thirty minutes, we stopped, and I could see a big valley and a view of gigantic mountain-like stairs of unusual colors from deep brown to light brown. That place is called La Gran Escalante. Six thousand years ago, that mountain range was formed.

We continued to Utah. We stopped in a town that looked like something out of a Western movie, like Laramie.it is called Kanab. The Western store was impressive (there is everything that cowboys might use).Across the street was the museum. They are both worth visiting.

From Kanab, we took road #9 towards Zion National Park. Before the park, we stopped at a ranch with horses, chickens, ducks, and large cows. The cows were huge and brown, all of them. Oh! They were bison.

From the ranch, we could see Zion National Park

Day 9

Zion National Park is part of the Colorado Plateau. According to the guide, six million years ago, everything was the sea; when the land came to the surface, it formed Navajo sandstone with the rivers. With the wind, the cliffs in Zion Canyon were formed. We walked through the canyons and rivers; we could see deer and turkeys up close. I was less tired and could enjoy it more since we were at a lower altitude. We were at the bottom of the canyon! The weather was pleasant, and seeing how the trees, plants, and animals moved with the breeze was relaxing.

Zion

Day 10

Highway 9 to Springdale is one of the most beautiful roads in the United States, as it goes from the top of the mountain to the bottom of Zion Canyon. After passing the first tunnel, we saw a mountain goat and toured Springdale. We continued west and could see the change in the ecosystem; everything was dry and hot again. I guessed it! We were returning to Las Vegas.

Once in Las Vegas, we walked along boulevard, better known as the Strip. We visited friendly hotels like El Bellagio, the fountains there had high jets that danced to the music. That was too crowded! There were more people there than in Walt Disney World in Orlando.

We also visited El Mirage, where I saw big ponds; I just wanted to grab the fish there in my mind.

That night, we stayed at the MGM casino. On the twenty-four floors!

Day 11

In the morning, we went downtown; Roberto(the brother of Ana) said, "This is where the great city of Las Vegas began." We strolled through the first casinos. Then we went to Mormon fort. Believe it or not, the Mormons were the first American citizens that settle in Las Vegas and the bankers who helped developed the city. Now it is filled with casinos.In the afternoon, we finally returned home; I would not mind the plane's noise or my fear. I was exhausted, I wondered what my next national park would be.

I learned that to serve better, one must accept things as they are. And beings as they are.

***

Wow, Scotty, what a trip. Didn't you go to the Rocky Mountains?

***

Yes, there I went, accompanied by my family from Mexico.

Do you want me to continue, Mitzi?

***

Yes, please continue.

Grand Canyon, Mesa Verde, and Zion National Parks

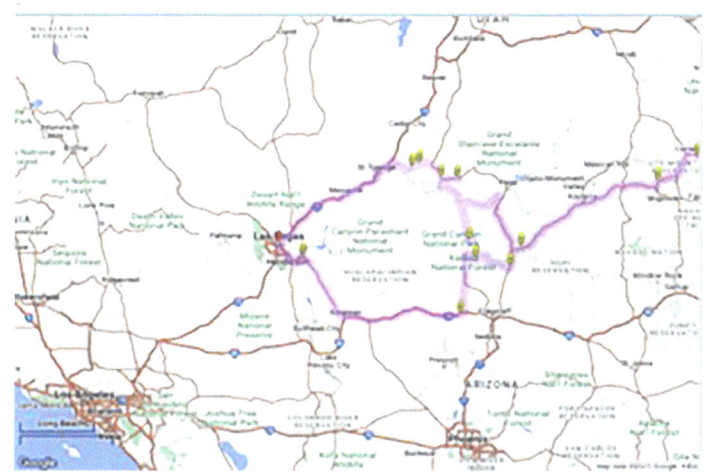

19

CHAPTER 3

US National Parks, Mountain West

One day Ana was extremely excited! She had made plans for us to travel again!

Mitzi our next journey began with a flight to Denver Colorado was told we were going to Denver with Roberto, and would meet our cousins from Mexico, AnaPau, and Abi. Little did I know it was the start of a great road trip, and we would see the Rockies, Grand Teton, and Yellowstone!

Day 1

That morning, I thought I was going for a walk in the park; imagine my surprise when I saw Roberto wake up early and load our luggage into his car. We drove to Fort Lauderdale, and then I realized I was at an airport. Oh, not the terror again! We flew for hours!

When we left the airport, I thought it would be like Vegas without grass, but to my surprise, there was grass. What joy! There we took a cab and went to the city center, and there we rented a huge car that was difficult to get into. So, Ana Had to pick me up into the big car and lift me safely to the ground.

Denver is a city on a large, flat plain. You can see the Rockies in the distance. Once we settled, we went to celebrate Roberto's birthday, and I was able to relax. I was already exhausted and had no strength for any fun.

Day 2

We got up early to walk, and after breakfast, we went west towards the Rockies, a colossal mountain range. We crossed beautiful valleys at the beginning and were almost immediately in Estes Park.

The city is crossed by a river called the Big Thompson River. I wanted to freshen up, but I was on duty. Further on in the middle of the town, was a beautiful dam with birds. (In my mind, I visualized myself chasing them.) We followed the road through Rocky Mountain National Park. The road was like what you see on TV. It was full of curves, like a snake. It is called Peak to Peak and is one of Colorado's scenic roads. The views were amazing. Suddenly I smelled a strange smell and there they were, deer! After taking photos from the view, we continued climbing into the tundra without trees. It was remarkably high, about 3300 meters. We were approaching the clouds, and we could see something white. We stopped the car, and I ran to see what it was. I skated! It was freezing. I was told it was ice and snow. Immediately I pushed Ana away from the snow because she could fall.

Rocky Mountain Tundra

Then, I began to feel intense winds.

I was at the summit!

The Alpine Visitor Center Ranger Station was crowded, wow! What a view! Everything seemed so small, and we were at the top.

We entered the center, and from there, you could see the beginning of the Colorado River. It was the same one I saw in the Grand Canyon. We had lunch there. We were overlooking a valley and tundra.

It was so high that we felt short of breath if we walked fast.(This happens because at high altitude is less oxygen in the air).

When we returned to the road, we saw a group of moose resting on the side of the road, and later we saw deer. Already down the valley towards Loveland, we continued through a canyon where we crossed the Big Thompson River again. The vegetation was dry and rocky. At last, we arrived in Loveland.

The hotel had a garden, and I enjoyed it. It was only for me to sniff, sniff. Suddenly, I smelled something. I took a deep breath and saw them. My heart pumped up, and I ran. They were rabbits! Somehow, they escaped from me, and only for the time being, I would say I misbehaved. I deserved the wake-up call.

"If you are going to do something you like and that gives you joy, do it because tomorrow is God's will, and you live only once."

Day 3

We headed northwest to Lander, Wyoming the next day exceedingly early, passing through Laramie and Rawlins. These places are very isolated. Ana thought Rawlins would be a wonderful place to eat. However, the city was so empty that we decided to continue and headed to Sweetwater Valley, where European immigrants gathered in caravans before leaving for Oregon.

The habitat on this road is mountainous and dry with rivers. The road changes a lot. It is semi-dry, there is a lot of wind, there are almost no trees, and the road is protected with wooden windbreaks. That is why it felt like the wind pushed the car. I ended up sleeping until I got to Lander.

Lander is a typical Western village with all the early twentieth-century buildings. A river crossed our hotel which was on the main avenue. We visited it, and I took the opportunity to leave my mark. At that moment, I noticed and advised Ana that I was smelling something from the other side of the river! It was a deer. It was beautiful. It was what they call donkey's ears deer.

Day 4

The following day, we headed towards a canyon near the city and saw a beautiful river with rapids. The place is called Sinks Canyon State Park, the river is Wind River. The Crow Indians call it Popo Agie River. This river flows through an underground limestone cavern and then emerges four hundred meters down the ravine but with more water flow. Scientists still need to find out where most of the water comes from. If you look east from the entrance to the cavern, you can appreciate the meadows where we arrived at Lander. From here, we went west through Shoshone territory. We started to climb the altiplano, and I could already feel the height. We got to climb up to 2,000 meters above sea level. As we headed towards the park, I noticed everyone was calm, watching the road. In front of us, we saw the peaks of the massive Grand Teton. These peaks measure four thousand meters above sea level. At the lake, we had lunch while viewing the Grand Teton. I asked Ana to take me for a walk, and we decided to walk to the lake; the water was cold. Suddenly, I felt someone watching me, but the view was magnificent, so I ignored my instincts. I let my guard down; I smelled something scary and pushed Ana back. It was a bear! A ranger approached us and asked us to leave quietly.

We had to continue our way towards Yellowstone, driving along the lake and enjoying the view from the car.

Finally, we entered Yellowstone Park, and as we passed a small lake, we saw water and steam fumaroles coming out. It was our first geyser; this is a pond with stinky water and bubbles. It is like a fountain, but with more pressure and hot water, like a natural pool of smelly water (sulfur water). I decided not to touch it and keep Ana away. However, there are more than seven colors in the background. The water was clear, and we appreciated the rainbow of colors. They say it is due to the bacteria and algae that inhabit those waters.

We followed the road, and suddenly, it felt like we were in the city. I mean, there was traffic, but I could smell something that reminded me of Zion National Park. A bison near us was resting in the middle of the road!

After fifteen minutes, we reached the villa and were assigned rooms. Fantastic! We had rooms on the second floor overlooking the forest. That night, we had dinner at Canyon Village. Ana decided not to drive, and we took the transport from the villa. Brrrrr, it was freezing! Even with my coat! The temperature drops very quickly after sunset. It was July, and it was minus 2 degrees Celsius. I was already exhausted. In my room, I found a toy bison. I was tired and just wanted to play with it. That is when I remembered what President Teddy Roosevelt said:

"Every being is a genius. You just must let it be expressed." He also said, "A life making mistakes is not only more honorable but also more useful than a life doing nothing."

Day 5

After a good rest, the next day, we woke up and saw another deer outside our building. I tried to chase him, but I remembered my obligations. I tried to catch the squirrel. In my mind, I made a calculation and concluded that he would climb the tree. Therefore, I did not do it.

****

Scotty, would you have been reprimanded if you did? I do not think so Mitzi, but I would feel bad; Rose, my trainer, taught us to respect wild animals.

That morning was cold, and the car had ice on the windows. We took the road north to visit the area because they said the wolves were there. I wanted to see them, but we were not lucky and missed them. Suddenly, we arrived at another village where we saw a hot rock formation called Mammoth Hot Springs. There is a caldera under the ground, and the water comes to the surface as a hot spring due to the heat that radiates out from a partially molten chamber of magma deep underground. The result of a cataclysmic volcanic explosion that occurred 600,000 years ago.(I am glad the volcano is dormant!!)

As they explained, water moves along an underwater "plumbing" system. The hot water rises through a system of small fissures, mixing with the hot carbon dioxide-laden gases rising from the magma chamber. The gasses dissolve in the hot water, creating a weak carbonic acid solution. That acidic solution dissolves substantial amounts of limestone through the rock layers and rises to the surface, forming hot springs. Water and soil exposed to the air expel carbon dioxide that escapes from mineral solutions. In other words, they include those strange rocks in the middle of the hot water called travertines. Just before I approached to smell it, Ana warned me not to put my nose close because it could burn me.

There are more than fifty hot springs in Mammoth Hot Springs.

I could see five terraces; the main terrace is the largest in the upper part and we also saw Palette Spring with so many colors. In the lower area are three main terraces Jupiter, Minerva, and Cleopatra. Liberty cap is one of the best-known hot rock cone formations. Its lift is eleven meters in the air. This hot cone was named in 1871 for its resemblance to the caps worn during the French Revolution. That is what they read to me.

According to the ranger, the internal pressure is high enough to push the water to a great height, allowing mineral deposits to accumulate in towers as they come to the surface.

Minerva Spring is another favorite geyser because of its wide range of colors and intricate travertine formations. Its activity has continued, and records have been kept about it since 1890. In the early 1900s, it was recorded that the spring was dry, but in 1951, it began to flow again up and still does up to this date,

On the lower terrace are several mounds; one is Orange Spring Mound, named for its color (Bacteria and algae create that color). The other bank is called Angel for its pure white color.

After walking in the area, we went west to return to the Villa.

In the afternoon, we went to see the waterfalls of Yellowstone River at the Grand Canyon of Yellowstone. These waterfalls are famous and appear in all the park pamphlets. They are beautiful. The canyon is bottomless in the bottom flows Yellowstone River, and further southeast are the rapids. These are the LeHardys rapids, where you can see trout jumping in the fall.

In the afternoon, we visited the museum in the village and watched a movie about volcanoes. I did not understand it, but I discovered that we were on top of a macro volcano.

Norris Geyser

Day 6

The following day, we went west and saw more geysers. At Norris Geyser, my eyes and nose hurt because of the sulfur. There are also beautiful hot water waterfalls. The place is also known as Geyser Valley. The boiling waters form a rainbow of colors with sunlight, and the Norris geyser basin is a geological area forged forever in chaos. This area is the hottest and most changeable area of Yellowstone, making it one of the most extreme environments on the face of the earth. Most of its thermal wells have temperatures above the boiling point of 93 degrees Celsius due to the area's elevation. I remembered the movie and hurried Ana to the car.

Traveling south, we entered the area where the most famous geyser is located. I saw some benches where many people sat watching a mound with a hole and a fumarole. They called it OLD FAITHFUL and explained that it was discovered in 1870 by the Washburn expedition. Old Faithful was named for its frequent and precise eruption. Its frequency is repeated every ninety minutes without fail.

Old Faithful can range in height from 30 to 55 feet, with an average of about 45.5 ft high. This has been the historical range of its recorded measurements. Rashes typically last between 1.5 and 5 minutes. Scientists estimate that the amount of water expelled is more than fourteen liters for a short duration of 1.5 minutes. For a time of 5 minutes, it's about thirty-two liters. The water temperature in the vent has been measured and is 95.6 degrees °C. The temperature of the steam was measured, and it goes above 176.7 degrees °C. Most of its thermal characteristics have temperatures above the boiling point of 93 degrees °C due to the area's elevation. I decided not to investigate that hole.

Old Faithful

We went to Yellowstone Lake in the afternoon, where they gave us a nice cabin. Wow, wow, there is a bison sleeping behind the place. Go, or I will bite you! The bison did not seem impressed, but I did a good solid growl!! GRRR.

Day 7

We were all exhausted and stayed at the lake lodge. According to a brochure, the hotel was built in the early 1900s, and Teddy Roosevelt slept there.

The lake is the largest body of water in Yellowstone National Park. It is 2357 meters above sea level and covers 350 square kilometers with 180 kilometers of coastline. The lake's average depth is 42 m, and its most remarkable depth is at least 120 meters.

Yellowstone Lake is North America's largest freshwater lake, at over 2100 meters over sea level.

The hotel is the oldest in the national park and was opened in 1891.

Yellowstone Lake

Day 8

The route from Cody to Yellowstone National Park is located towards the East. It is considered the most picturesque of the five gates of the park. With these views, I said goodbye to the place with its depths and surface still in constant movement.

I remember my friend Dr. in physics Luis Parra, said: "Every effect has its cause, and every reason has its development; this is the result and consequence of one of my previous thoughts, actions, or intentions.

Everything is dual since everything has opposites and cannot exist without them. It would be best to modify its polarity by going to its opposite to change something."

****

Scotty is this done by earth, animals, and Humans?

****

Mitzi, Yes! However,

I think that some humans do not believe it.

We continued along the road to Wapiti Valley, where Buffalo Bill founded the city of Cody, Wyoming. As we approached the town, we observed the Absaroka Mountain range in the distance. This is one of the most scenic roads because it crosses bridges and tunnels around ravines and rivers. The view is magnificent. We passed through several tunnels and gorges along the route, admiring the landscapes and observing the river.

In Cody, we visited the Buffalo Bill Museum. There, we saw how pioneers began to settle in the region from the late 1700s to the early 1900s. Also, we saw the exhibits where they showed the colonization of Europeans emigrants intrude upon natives' land breaking the treaty sign and modify in 1851.As is written in one of the exhibits:

"This war did not spring up on our land: war was brought upon us by the children of the Great Father who came to take our land without a price, and who, in our land, do a great many evil things…This war has come from robbery-form stealing of our land." - *written by Spotted Tail*

From Cody we went to the town of Thermopolis. Mountains surround this city: the Bridger Mountains to the southeast, the Owl Creek Mountains to the southwest, the Big Horn Mountains to the northeast, and the Absaroka Range, from which we came, to the northwest. Thermopolis Township is the southernmost part of the Bighorn Basin. At the city's northern end is a unique geological formation remarkably similar in shape to a volcano. It is approximately 1829 meters high and is the highest area near Thermopolis. The city is named for its hot springs and massive travertine terraces formed over centuries by waterfalls of hot mineral water. Hot Springs State Park appears to be dying. Big Spring produced 49.2 million liters of water per day in 1896 (when the Indians sold it to the pioneers); now, it only produces 13.5 million liters daily, and the cause is still unknown.

That afternoon, we stayed inside the park at the first hotel in the city. Ana was upset because I had fun getting into the pool to cool off. It was a small pool. They called it a spring. Nearby were more hot springs and terraces. I do not think they allow dogs to be there, but I could not stand it.

Thermopolis has the Wyoming Dinosaur Center and conducts paleontology excavations. In the area, there is a visitor center with a museum. In this museum, I saw for the first time vast bones of the dinosaurs, Camarasaurus, and the Supersaurus. (I wanted to take them and hide them underground.) I do not understand why they exposed them.

Day 9

From Thermopolis, we started southeast, passing through the Shoshone Canyon. We follow the road to Cheyenne.

On the way, when we saw the hills, we began to see antelopes and watched a storm approach. I was impressed as the black clouds advanced through the prairie.

Cheyenne is the state capital and the largest city in Wyoming. When we arrived, they were preparing the city for Pioneer Day. As in the nineteenth century, it is a rodeo festival, where cows are loose and enter the town freely. They travel through the city to Pioneers Park.

Day 10

We visited Cheyenne and toured two museums: one in the city center and another in Pioneers Park. For half a day, we returned to Denver and visited downtown in the afternoon.

Denver Airport

Day 11

It was already the day to return home, and I slept two days in a row!

Remembering the valleys, mountains, and meadows, I began to perceive how everything has an effect; we must accept and not change. What do you think about it, Mitzi?

***

"Scotty, you are right. You must go by the current until you reach the shore if you do not drown. The way forward is your goal. The past was there. Why didn't I see you when we could not go far because of quarantine?"

Map of Rocky Mountain, Grand Teton, and Yellowstone National Parks

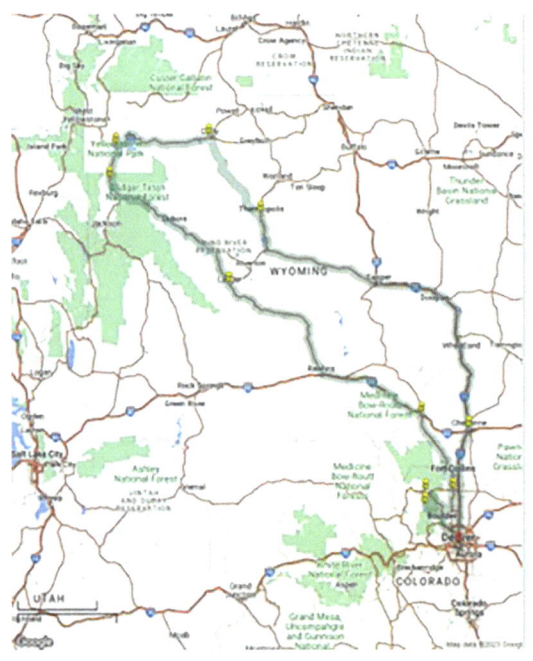

CHAPTER 4

MIAMI TO COOPERSTOWN—TRIP DURING COVID

Ana was apprehensive when we heard about a human disease called COVID-19 on the news. The precautions we had to take were wearing a mask and plastic gloves, using soap and water every time we entered or left the house, spraying me with a special liquid for dogs that had the smell of cologne and alcohol so that I did not carry the germ in my fur, and washing my paws with warm water. Do you remember Mitzi? That cleaner thing did not matter because I got an extra massage on my belly and back. That pleased me. I did not know that germs could be devastating and kill many people. This virus caused a global pandemic.

So, Ana researched a place where we could hide from COVID. She found a town in Upstate New York called Cooperstown. That was the place where we went to hide from COVID. Roberto rented a country house on the outskirts of that town.

Day 1

On August 13, we started driving north on I-95. I was in the car for several hours, admiring the road. (I had no choice).

We stopped in Georgia for a quick lunch near Kingsland. Later, we continued Highway 26 to Columbia, South Carolina, where we rested in a hotel.

Day 2

The following day, we headed northwest of Interstate 20 into the mountains. Then, we started to see the Appalachian Mountains Range. This part is known as the Smoky Mountains because there is always fog in the morning. It was so beautiful. We saw diverse kinds of pine trees. The day was cloudy, and the road and the weather were pleasant. We stopped for breakfast and then set on the road to Roanoke, Virginia. We turned north on Interstate 81, where we had practically crossed the mountain range, and you could see the valleys in the distance. We were able to view the George Washington Jefferson National Forest.

I wanted to walk, so I asked them to get me out of the car, so we stopped at Natural Bridge in Virginia. (This site is a geological natural arch carved out of limestone by cedar creek, is 90 feet in length and 215 feet in height, it is located in the southern Shenandoah valley , We thought in this site includes a historical hotel with Monacan Indian village and a wax museum). about eating at the hotel, however, it was closed because of COVID. We continued north, stopping at a gas station for a quick lunch. With COVID, humans tried to have as little contact with each other as possible, but I noticed that many of them were not paying attention. From one state to another, the instructions changed. In some, the instructions were for all to wear masks; in others, it was your choice. We passed into Maryland practically without realizing it, and when entering Pennsylvania, we stopped and rested in Harrisburg.

(Farmers Market Hershey)

Day 3

Before entering New York State, we went to several farmers' markets on the road and stopped in Hershey to buy food, kibble, and chocolates. On leaving, we visited Scranton, where we had lunch and toured downtown and its university. Upon entering New York State, we headed straight to Cooperstown, as we had to stay on the property for fifteen days in quarantine. People visiting the state, by law, had to report daily to the New York government their temperature and health because of COVID-19.

After two nights, we finally arrived at the property we rented. It was on a hill just outside of Cooperstown. The property was huge and had three acres for me to run around on and explore. The house was old from the nineteenth century. It had four bedrooms, a porch, a large kitchen, and a vast dining room. In that place, I could smell different animals: squirrels, marmots, deer, and coyotes.

Cooperstown house

Day 4 to Day 19

For the first fifteen days, we explored the entire house. In the mornings, we would go up the hill. We would walk around the house in the afternoons, and in the evenings, we would walk around the house again.

One day, we found an archaeological stone. We found a small Indian mill that looked like it has been used to grind corn or file an arrowhead. This place was a site of pow wow or a meeting place of several tribes of the Iroquois Confederacy (Mohawk, Oneida, Onondaga, Cayuga, and Seneca). At the end of the glacial lake, before the river flows in downtown Cooperstown, there is a stone called Council Rock, and legend has it that the Iroquois Confederacy met there.

Small mill

Cooperstown is also known for the Baseball Hall of Fame. It has bat factories and national youth championships are held there every year. That year, they did not allow it because of COVID.

Day 20

The day came when the quarantine ended, and we all had cabin fever, especially Roberto. So, we all went out to tour the city. We had breakfast in front of Lake Otsego. From there, we walked around the lake to a picturesque village called Cherry Valley, founded in 1739 by the Scots and English. It is one of the oldest villages in this region.

Days 21_56

One day in September, my friend Bellini visited us after quarantine. It was fun to see him again. We played and went to the hill. We could not run like before, but we chased squirrels and rolled across the grass.

Ana and Margaret (the owner of Bellini) took us to the famous Baseball Hall of Fame.

Bellini explained that the game consists of hitting a ball and running like crazy, they will run in circles returning to the place where they hit the ball, just like us when we drop it so that our humans' friend can through it again. Players try to catch the ball; some of them are good, like us, but some are not. He also told me that when Margaret takes him to watch the games, he watches for a while and falls asleep. It is boring just watching and not being able to play.

We entered the museum with human statues and balls that we could not touch or smell, and we visited all the rooms with different figures and old photos. This is how the players remember each other.

Baseball Hall of Fame

Cooperstown has breweries and distilleries where you can try bourbon. That is where the bourbon Triple Play is famous.

Another day, we went to Glimmerglass State Park. We walked through the park and visited Ostego Bay, which is such a beautiful place, and the lake water was nice. It was a bit cold, but you could swim. As expected, Bellini did not get involved. In the park, we saw a dam made by beavers on the smaller lake, and we were not allowed to explore.

Glimmerglass Park

We left the park, circled the lake, and had lunch at Blue Mingo. We could see the lake from the west side. Then, we went to the Fenimore Art Museum, where Indigenous artifacts are collected.

There, I saw the stones! Just like the ones I found in the house. The museum also has exhibits of folk art from the region. We visited vineyards, which was fun because we could tour them and their lakes. Ana and Margaret tasted the wines, and Bellini and I delighted in the charcuterie, cheese, and bread. We visited a different state park each week, walked through the woods, and saw other streams and trees.

Hill in the house- Cooperstown

I noticed that every day, it was colder, and the leaves began to fall and change their color. Also, I thought that the squirrels here were bombarding us with pinecones. They collect them to store because it is their food for the winter, but it seemed to me that they bombed me, and I had to hide from the attack of pinecones that they threw towards me.

One day, the temperature dropped to 0 degrees Celsius. It began to get colder and shorter days. We tried to make the most by visiting state parks. We saw an apple mill in Fly Creek where they make cider.

In Cooperstown, I learned that the famous writer Fenimore Cooper lived here. He became extremely popular with his Hawkeye stories and his adventures as a hunter in this region in the eighteenth century.

My favorite walk was to go to the farmer's markets there, and they always gave me cheese or ham treats.

The excellent stuff ended, and we had to go home. I had to leave the three acres where I used to run, explore, and jump. I was the king of the hill, chasing squirrels and marmots, but not coyotes, with whom I did not mess.

Day 57

The return day was approaching, so we packed up and headed south to Pennsylvania. Ana told me we would stop to visit the Gettysburg

National Military Battlefield Park. I did not know what that meant, but I did know the words national park and I knew them well. The term national park I knew very well. Those are parks to walk in and see different animals. Some parks are in mountains, others are in swamps, some have rivers, and some have forests or are in the ocean. So, I was excited to see that place.

Gettysburg is important because a decisive battle occurred there, whatever that means. The north of the United States of America won, and the country was not divided. The enslaved people were freed, and democracy triumphed. (That means I can walk and explore because we are free.)

The place is beautiful, full of hills; it seems incredible that humans kill each other for strange ideas that I still do not understand. We saw canyons and different fences, such as the Wyoming windbreaker; they explained that these were used as barriers to stop horses and soldiers. Here, 23,000 Union soldiers and 28,000 Confederate soldiers died. It is where there were most human losses on American soil. We walked up the hill and climbed the mountain, visiting different sites. It was exhausting but fascinating, and the valleys already had different autumn colors.

After visiting the park, we went to Maryland and stayed near Washington, DC, in Rockville, where we rested.

Day 58

Roberto had breakfast with his clients. We rested in the hotel until Roberto arrived. At mid-morning, we left the hotel to head south, taking the I-95 road toward Charleston. The road was challenging and tedious because it rained all the time. We stayed overnight at Albemarle Point, across the river from downtown Charleston.

Day 59

In the north, near the mountains, you miss the ocean. I was so excited to see the sea and the oaks, I rolled in the grass and scared away the ibises nearby.

That same day, we visited downtown Charleston.

Battery Street, Charlestown

It is an old southern city. We went to Oyster Point, White Point, and Battery Street. We could not visit the inside of the museums because of COVID restrictions. I was told Charleston and Savannah were not burned in the Civil War. That is why these cities are so beautiful with the southern mansions of the nineteenth century. The bay in Charleston is impressive and massive. From it, three rivers go to the Atlantic Ocean. These are from north to south: Wando River, Cooper River, and Ashley River. The latter flows into a delta.

Roberto continued driving down Highway 7 toward Savannah, and I fell asleep and woke up because the road was paved. When I woke up, I was in Savannah! I saw the old houses with the oaks full of moss typical of this area.

After lunch in downtown Savannah, we headed south to Florida and stopped to rest at the World Golf Village Hotel outside St. Augustine. We walked around the hotel until I got tired, as traveling for days in the car was exhausting. We did not stop because of COVID at the Florida animal service center for the deaf and blind (FDBA), this is where the famous service dogs' school is. It is where dogs are trained for blind people or as soldiers.

Day 60

We finally got home. I miss you, my friends, especially you, Mitzi.

We hid from the virus, and we learned to contemplate life, accept what we have lived, and move forward. Everything is possible if you set your goals.

Love yourself and move on. Just have faith because, with your will, you will reach your goal.

Morningside

Map from Miami to Cooperstown

CHAPTER 5

The Riviera Maya

I will tell you about my grand adventure on the Riviera Maya.

Day 1

Ana was excited and said, "Today, you will see something you cannot imagine." That was very strange because we usually go to the beach on weekends rather than Fridays. A friend of Ana's picked us up in her car with our luggage. Oh no! It was the airport. We flew to Cancun. I hope the flight will last only a brief time. I am terrified of flying. As soon as we got on the plane, I decided to sleep. After two hours, Ana said, "Welcome to my country," and we disembarked.

When we went outside, I was ready to leave my mark but was so excited that I forgot. Everything smelled so different from Miami. The streets had another smell; there was more noise and movement.

I met Abi and her daughter Ana Pau. They are Ana's relatives. They are also genuinely friendly. At the airport, we rented a minivan. We arrived at the hotel, where we were given a room. From there, we ate at the Piola, an open-air restaurant. In Mexico, only service dogs are accepted in restaurants, so you must see the list on www.dogfriendlycancun.mx, for all the places dogs are welcome.

In the afternoon, we went to the Pier of Cancun, where we began the tour of the hotel zone. We stopped at the Mirador Playa los Delfines. Woof, there is the sea! I was told I could not go to the beach. I was not welcome there because they did not accept pets. How disappointing this was! We returned to the city and had Mexican food at EMARA 1. Then we went to rest at the hotel.

Day 2

We got up early, but it was late because I was used to eastern time, not Cancun Time. We went for a walk, and I could not find a lovely place to leave my mark. All those smells were different, and there were humans walking around; there were a lot of small shops on the street with handmade crafts in distinct colors, all of which distracted me.

Ana texted Abi, and we agreed to meet in the parking lot. There, we all got in the car. We were on the Cancun-Chetumal Highway, and after fifteen minutes, we stopped at Oxxo to drink coffee. I took advantage and left my mark there. I began to feel the heat of this place; thank goodness the car had air conditioning. The girls did not stop talking; we stopped two times to put gas in the van. After three hours of driving, we saw water and were all amazed at what we saw. It was a lagoon with distinct colors of blue, ranging from dark blue to emerald. It has seven assorted colors. This lagoon was called Bacalar.

Bacalar is also the name of the town where we arrived; it is located on a hill and has a beautiful square, a government building, markets, shops, and a church. Here, too, there is a fort from colonial times. It is called San Felipe and was completed in 1733. It defended the area from pirates approaching the coast looking for the dye stick.(dye stick is a saw grass or bamboo used for writing in colonial times).

Upon leaving the fort, they decided to rent a boat and take a boat ride. Then, we looked for food in a grocery store, and from there, we went to a private house at the lagoon. As the girls boarded the boat, I cooled my paws on the lagoon's shore.

Bacalar

The boat ride was enjoyable. We could appreciate the town of Bacalar. And on the other side, you could see the shallow waters with beautiful shades of blue. In the distance, we could observe stromatolites; according to the captain, these microbes create colonies and form rocky sediments over time. They are bioconstructions that continue to grow and form round shapes. These stromatolites are considered the oldest forms of living things. According to the Autonomous University of Mexico (UNAM), stromatolites are becoming extinct because of excessive tourism. That is, the Lagoon is dying because excess use is destroying the natural equilibrium of the lagoon since the organism cleans the carbon monoxide oxygenating the lagoon naturally.

The captain stopped the boat in a bay called Cenote de las Brujas. The cousins immediately jumped into the water, and I jumped in to save them even though the water was bottomless. I did not know I was jumping into a sinkhole, and I did not know what to do. At that moment, Ana jumped in and took me out. Then, she permitted me to eat on the boat and praised me for my heroic efforts.

Afterward, we arrived at the east side of the lagoon where the pirates used to hide. There, the water is shallow and clear. I could see the fish and managed to touch the bottom of the lagoon. Finally, we returned to the port from which we left. I was already so tired that I just fell asleep.

I did not notice when we arrived in Mahaual. It is a village of anglers and is by the sea. The hotel where we stayed was on the beach. Upon entering the lobby, I had to growl and show the big boxer who was the boss. We toured the village at night and watched the sea waves hitting the beach.

Day 3

The following day, we saw the sunrise on the sea. It was beautiful.

We left for Puerto Aventura, but before, we stopped at Akumal, another fishing port and the entrance to the biosphere with the same name. It is a protected area to conserve the delicate ecosystem. Akumal has one of the most picturesque bays in the Riviera Maya.

Before arriving at Puerto Aventura, we stopped in Muyil, where there was an archaeological zone dating from the classic period. Its architecture was Peten-type. Muyil was a town where maritime trade developed. Nearby is the Sian Ka'an reserve and its lagoon with the same name. It was worth seeing.

Muyil

Do not laugh, Mitzi. Names in Maya are complicated to pronounce.

We arrived in Puerto Aventura at dusk. The hotel was a small boutique type. Wow, what a cozy place! I was so excited that I passed by the room and went straight to the beach. I dipped into a small natural cove in front of the room.

Puerto Aventura.

Before dinner, we walked down the street, and I saw a rare animal called an agouti. It seemed like a small capybara but had a strong smell and could jump up to two meters. It escaped me! For dinner, we went to a market in Puerto Aventura.

At that place, everyone walked with their pets. The square had an aquarium with dolphins, sea lions, and manta rays. After dinner, we returned to the hotel, and once in the room, I could not take it anymore and went to bed early.

Day 4

The next day, we saw the sunrise on the beach near the hotel. On the way back, I saw agouties,' and of course, I went to the little cove to take a dip. We went to Coba before I had breakfast because I was hungry after so much exercise.

The archaeological zone of Coba is a Mayan center of the classic and postclassic period that goes from 250AD until the arrival of the Spanish conquistadors around 1570 AD. It is located b in an area between five lagoons and is believed to have been a commercial city with more than 50,000 inhabitants at its peak at the end of the classic Period (900 AD). This city has the highest pyramid on the peninsula. It is forty-eight meters high, called Nohoch Mul. Coba covered an area of eighty square meters. There were fifteen complexes of houses or villas, and all were linked by sacbeob or Mayan roads. (white roads made with limestone that shine with the moon). The area with the most considerable number of temples between Lake Coba and Lake Macanxoc, called Nohoch Mul. We decided to visit the whole area by pedicabs. (Good thing they had them available).

Ixma o Nohoch Mul   **Pedicab**

As we were in the Cenotes area, we visited them. Boca del Puma is an open cenote in the middle of the jungle. From there, we went to another cenote called Verde, which was more profound and had stalactites and tree roots entering the water. As we were leaving this place, at the road's junction, we saw kingfisher nests hanging from the trees, butterflies, and several chachalacas.

From there, we headed to Puerto Morelos. That city is also picturesque and was founded in the early twentieth century. Before Cancun existed, it was already a commercial port. The Puerto Morelos National Reef Park is part of the second-largest reef in the world. On its beaches, one can observe the nests of turtles. They did not let me approach so as not to disturb them. The church in the square dates from 1898 and is dedicated to St. Joseph the Worker. This is a typical coastal town, although it is already losing its charm.

Day 5

We decided to get up at dawn and go to Punta Isla Blanca. which is north of Puerto Juárez. After traveling for thirty-five minutes, we arrived at the port. (This is the fishing village where you can catch the cheapest ferry to Islas Mujeres, which is a beautiful island with crystal clear waters and stunning beaches). Passing Puerto Juarez is Punta Sam, and Punta Isla Blanca is at the end of the road.

This punta is magnificent. On one side is the Caribbean Sea, and on the other, the lagoon. At the tip, you can see the Contoy Island National Park and the Isla Blanca lagoon on the west side. You can also see the Chacmuchuch biosphere, which is still virgin, and to the northeast, enclosing the lagoon is the Chacmochuk key which is not populated.

These waters are shallow, and I could swim, run, and enjoy it here. I spent the whole morning enjoying the beach.

On the way back, we stopped by the archaeological zone El Meco, a city of the classic period dedicated to the naval trade of fishing and the commerce of salt.

In front is a magnificent church with a spectacular view. The church is dedicated to the Virgin Mary.

If you can, do not miss it because, in the background, Isla Mujeres is distinguished.

Day 6

The last day was dedicated to getting to know Cancun well. We went to the hotel zone, where we visited the city museum and the archaeological site, El Rey. The latter is from the early classic Maya period (250AD -500AD). Its inhabitants were dedicated to commercializing salt and fishing.

In the area, there are forty-seven structures. Building #2 stands out as the tomb of a high-ranking person because of the clothes, bracelets, and copper ax that were found.

After leaving the archaeological site, we went to cool off at Punta Nizuc, where the coral beach is assigned to pets.

Day 7

That morning, we went to downtown Cancun to a handicraft market called Mercado 28. After buying the gifts for the house, we left for the airport, and within two hours, we were back in Miami. So, I started thinking:

How different our life was from that of the Mayans, who were so attached to nature that they kept that respect and maintained their ecosystem. Hopefully, the new generations of Mexicans do not destroy those habitats that are the lungs of Mesoamerica. The Yucatan rainforest is an extremely fragile ecosystem.

***

Let me see if I understood Scotty, according to the Mayans, the word for roads is sacbe or sakbej, and everyone has a sacbe to travel. You must start by loving yourself because you must fill the years with life, not the life with years. You only learn from the past to travel to a better future and enjoy every moment.

***

You are right, Mitzi. See you tomorrow? I want to tell you what I saw in Yucatan.

Punta Nizuc

Map of the Riviera Maya

CHAPTER 6

Yucatan, The Emerald Coast

"Hi, Scotty! Are we going to our favorite place in the park? And when we get there, would you tell me another story about your travels?"

"Yes, Mitzi, let's go." This time I will tell you about another trip we took to see many things that my human, Ana, wanted to see. But you know she cannot go anywhere without me!"

***

One morning, Ana told me. "I am planning to visit the northern part of the Yucatan Peninsula and would like to know where a large colony of flamingos live. (Those are pink birds with rare beaks and long legs.) We will prepare to go to Yucatan. Our trip was planned for.

February 2020. when we traveled. That was a year when humans changed their way of life; they stopped driving all the time, and most stayed in their homes. They began wearing masks to cover their noses and mouths.

Ana told me. "Difficult times are coming; let's leave everything ready just in case."

The Yucatan Peninsula is divided into three states: Campeche, Yucatan, and Quintana Roo.

We took a flight to Cancun in the state of Quintana Roo. There we rented a car. Ana had planned a good vacation. First, we would see Celestún and follow the entire Emerald Coast to relax, and then we would detour to Mérida to get to know it. We would return by the east side to Temozón to eat a good cecina (broiled seasoned beef) before flying back to Miami.

Day 1

After spending two days in bank management, we left Cancun early. We went to get a coffee for Ana at Starbucks and an ice cream for me. We took the old road to Valladolid. This road is the old road that passes through all the villages. It is more fun, as it is full of different smells and landscapes, and the route passes small, picturesque villages and churches.

In Valladolid, we stopped at the municipal government palace, where on the second floor, there are murals from colonial times; from there, we went to breakfast at the Zací cenote (a sinkhole) in the center of the city and enjoyed the park. Then we went to the convent San Bernardino de Siena, where you can appreciate the frescoes dating from the sixteenth century and see the Zis-Ha cenote another sinkhole in its gardens.

Later, we went to Uayma, where we visit the former convent of San Antonio de Padua and its church. They told me to behave because we were entering the temple. We appreciated the smell of candles, as well as incense. The church was so clean! It also had a beautiful façade.

The next city was Izamal, known as the Yellow City. As they explained, all the houses are painted yellow in honor of the Vatican. Its church is at the top of a pyramid (Templo Mayor). That place was already a big Mayan city from 500 BC, with over eighty buildings. A Mayan priest named Zamna lived there. He was the one who invented Mayan books and the use of henequen. (The plant that is used to make rope with its fibers).

The Franciscan convent above the pyramid is dedicated to St. Anthony of Padua, and it is the second-largest atrium in the world. It has seventy-five arches which enclose the esplanade of 7,806 square meters.

It is impressive! To be able to see the church, you must climb the steps of the pyramid.

As it was already late, Ana decided to eat at Teya. a henequen hacienda and founded in 1683. It is located on the outskirts of the capital of Yucatan Merida. Teya is now a hotel restaurant where, apart from its beautiful gardens, there are deer and animals from the region. If you have time, do not miss it.

Finally, we took the peripheral road of Mérida and headed toward Celestún. After an hour and a half in the car, I smelled the sea, and we entered a small village. Then Ana said: "The Ría Celestún is protected as a UNESCO biosphere. It is part of a vast mangrove corridor northwest of the peninsula. Fresh water from underground aquifers has its outlet at these sites, making the biosphere reserve humid. Its mangroves, dunes, and low jungles are home to flamingos." The area is a resting place for migratory species. Although the site is known for its pink flamingos, the beaches and blue water of the gulf attract visitors.

I could not take it anymore; I wanted to go to the sea to cool off!

We arrived that afternoon in Celestun. The house was in the center, and the smell of the sea was next to the beach. After unpacking, we went to the beach to dive and play with the waves. Suddenly, I saw a kind of boat on the beach; they were fishing boats that are adapted for tourists to take them safely to the estuary.

Ana spoke with the people in charge and agreed to go the next day to visit the estuary.

That night we rode a motorcycle taxi and visited the whole town.

Day 2

The next day, we settled into one of those fishing boats and visited the estuary. The boat sailed along the coast until it entered a vast channel. Upon entering the estuary, we could see the pink birds, eagles, and cormorants, and we also observed the Petenes (typical mangroves of the area that grow in brackish waters and are nourished by the cenotes found in the estuaries and in the lagoons that go from Campeche to Progreso). On the way back, we saw old houses of abandoned salt haciendas.

After relaxing on the beach that afternoon, we visited the haciendas, salt flats, and then the fishing port.

Day 3

The Costa Esmeralda begins in Progreso and ends in Dizlam de Bravo. We had to cross lagoons and swamps to reach the coast before getting to that tongue of land, just before Xcambo, where a meteorite fell. The meteorite entered, according to experts, sixty-five million years ago. It was the one that caused the extinction of the dinosaurs and formed a crater 180 kilometers in diameter. It is currently a tourist place and can be visited.

Day 4

We headed south to visit Dizlam de Bravo—a fishing village with marinas. On the way back took the road towardsXcambo, we saw salt lagoons, flamingos, and seabirds. After crossing the lagoon, we headed to the archaeological site of Xcambo.

Salt was and still is exploited and traded by the Mayans and their descendants. It was a wonderful experience. Although I knew about archaeological sites, I had never been allowed to climb pyramids. Those narrow, twenty-centimeter-high steps forced me to jump each step. Then I realized that I could go up diagonally. That is how I climbed my first pyramid. This one was small at twelve meters. Upstairs, I saw the sea in the distance and saw a Catholic chapel with its little altar and flowers. The guide explained that this was how the Franciscan fathers converted the Mayans.

Day 5

We left the Emerald Coast and visited villages. We took Road 172 to Sacapuc. In Sacapuc, we saw a horse ranch where charros are trained. The Ranch has a typical structure of the colonial era with stables, gardens, and a church.

From there, we arrived at Baca, its church is from the seventeenth century.

Finally, we arrived in Cholul and stayed there in the suburbs of Merida, the capital of Yucatan. Merida is a Spanish colonial city with old Spanish charm and a French influence. Yucatan was one of the leading exporting regions for sisal, which it was very profitable in the French intervention in Mexico 1864.

Paseo Montejo

The Mayan and History Museum in Mérida explains this part of the region's history. It is worth visiting. We toured the city's tourist attractions, such as Paseo Montejo, the Convents, and the Museum of Concal. Paseo Montejo is lined by the old colonial houses and is in French style. We also visited the convent in Concal, which is an old mission. The churches and convents of Yucatan were built as forts, as they were at war with the Mayans for many years.

The Mayans fought against the landowners who called themselves Yucatecans. These battles were called the Caste War of Yucatán (1847-1901). The Yucatecans had long maintained political and economic control of the region. A long war ensued between them. In the northeast were the sisal and cotton ranchers and traders, and in the southwest, the independent Maya. Among them, they made frequent raids.

In the afternoon, we went to the archaeological site of Dzibilchaltun. This area is from the classical period (AD 500). It was a shopping center. Its most famous structure is that of the seven dolls. One can watch the sunrise through the temple gate during the spring equinox. We walk along the sacbe towards the Xlakah cenote, passing ruins and Mayan stelae.

Day 6

We took the 176 road to continue visiting and having breakfast in Motul. There is a dish called huevos motuleños, two eggs on top of a toasted corn tortilla topped with refried beans and bathed in spicy tomato sauce. (Neither you nor I, Mitzi, can eat it because it has beans and hurts us.) The city was founded in the eleventh century and was ruled by Pech Mayans. It was also a colonial city conquered by Francisco de Montejo, and in its church, there are exciting frescoes from that time. Two hours from there is Tizimin. This small town is famous because its church dates from the sixteenth century and is dedicated to the Magi. From there, we turned southwest to take Road 295 until it deviated from the archaeological site Ek Balam. They did not let me in at Ek Balam because.

It is extremely dangerous it is the habitat of their wild animals that I could attract with my smell. I stayed outside with Ana, and we saw part of the museum and a craft market. In the museum, we learned about the archaeological city Ek Balam. It was founded by Coch Cal Balam, who came from the east and the predecessor of the Cochacal Balams rebellion against the Yucatecans. The aristocracy of the Cupul family dominated the region, and the city grew from AD 770 to 1150. The Acropolis is enormous. It is an oval palace and a façade. Its Mayan arch can be seen from the parking lot.

We ate in Temozón and went to Cancun because it was already late.

Day 7

The flight left at 10:00 a.m. We got up and went straight to the airport to return to Miami. While waiting for the flight, I started thinking:

I must remember all the beautiful things I saw and remember the lessons. They will help me and guide me in the future, and I must enjoy every moment.

It should not be taken for assumptions; if there is doubt, it must be clarified. Belief leads us down the wrong path. Being authentic makes you trustworthy and it is the formula for reaching the goal that you set yourself.

***

"Scotty, you are getting it!

Did not you see Chichen-Itza?" I know you are going to ask that Mitzi!!But it is late so, I will tell you about it tomorrow.

Map of Yucatan, The Emerald Coast

CHAPTER 7

MAYAN WORLD

It was almost New Year's Eve, and Ana asked Roberto about their Christmas plans. I stopped and listened to see if they said the keyword *"travel."* So, what do you think? Roberto mentioned that Aninha, his daughter, wanted to visit us. He asked if she wanted to come to Florida or go to Yucatan. She preferred to go to Yucatan.

Ana began to investigate and planned the whole trip.

On this trip, we traveled to the Mayan world and visited five cities, three colonial towns, and two biospheres in three states. That is, we went around the Yucatan Peninsula.

Day 1

Now, I was ready to travel by plane to the Mayan world. I woke early and walked for an hour to get tired at the airport. I boarded the plane and settled into Ana's arms for the flight.

Upon landing, I went straight to the veterinarian's office to greet them and get approval. In less than ten minutes, we were already picking up the car. This time, the entire process was swift.

We arrived at the hotel and waited for Aninha and Leaf to arrive. They were coming from Norway. At sunset, we went to celebrate Christmas Eve near the hotel.

Day 2

The next day, we took the opportunity to leave at seven in the morning for Chichen-Itza. We wanted to be among the first to enter. Ana told Roberto and Aninha to pull out of the car and make the entrance line while we looked for a place to park. (The Site was Pack!!) After fifteen minutes of driving around the parking lot, we finally made it. I had to show all my credentials and medical permission to enter with Ana. After they checked everything, the administrator radioed, and we managed to get through.

Ana called Roberto, and we met at the ball court. From there we visited the famous pyramid of Kukulkan. It is the pyramid where you can see a shadow at the equinoxes that comes down as a feathered serpent at dusk. If you applaud, an echo reproduces the noise of the quetzal. (If you want to hear it go to YouTube quetzal bird sounds). That song deceived me; I could not see or smell the quetzals. That noise drove me crazy when I heard it. Then Ana clarified to me that it was the effect of the pyramid. When she applauded, the sound from the pyramid returned like the song of the quetzal. The incredible thing was to hear that when the Mayan priests climbed the stairs, sounded like drops of water in the pyramid. I could not check it because climbing is forbidden. It is impressive how square it is, the sounds and shadows it reproduces. As mentioned by the guide, this pyramid has ninety-one steps on each side, which adds up to 364 steps. The platform is 365, which represents the days of the year.

From there, we went to the oldest area and the sacred cenote, where we could observe the pyramid of the warriors and the observatory. At the top of the observatory, there is a round-shaped sundial. They used it to study Venus and the movement of the stars and the moon. The

Mayan priests managed to calculate the correct times for their crops. This pyramid is also known as the snail pyramid because of its shape.

This archeological site is so big that one needs at least four hours to appreciate it as we did. I hope you get to go and consider spending four to five hours in Chichen-Itza if you want to visit.

Kukulkan

The Observatory

The pyramid tour was fascinating, but we finally got tired, so we returned to the car and ate at Acanceh. In front of the restaurant, next to the pyramid in the city's center, you can see Mayan masks from the Puuc period that goes from around 800 AD to1000 AD).

After lunch, we continued to Mayapan, the city that arose when Chichen-Itzá was in decline and had trade with Tulum. There is a sacbe in a straight line that connects the two cities. Today, guides lead tourists along these roads.

Mayapan is from the classic to the post-classic period (from 800 to 1547) and is also a walled city. It has more than 4,000 structures in 4.2

square kilometers. The temple of Kukulkan is also called the castle. It is the largest in this archaeological zone. It allows me to climb there, but neither Ana nor I dare to go to the top of the pyramid because it is nine floors high. Nearby are the Temple of the Warriors and the Temple of the Painted Niches where there are frescoes. There is also a temple as an observatory.

You can find more information here: www.en-yucatan.com.mx. If you want to visit it, consider staying two to five hours.

We left Mayapan very tired and headed towards Muna, where we only entered the church. According to a tourist pamphlet, the convent dates from the sixteenth century and was one of the first in the region.

At dusk, we finally arrived at Hotel Resort De Uxmal to rest.

Day 3

Uxmal is a Mayan city of the classic period and the Puuc culture (see www.inah.gob.mx, for more detail on the Mayan periods and the Puuc culture). It is easily distinguished because here, the pyramids have only one staircase facing east and in Mayapan there are four staircases, one for each cardinal point. It is impressive when you start the tour, and the first thing you see is the Magician's pyramid. This city was founded in the sixth century of our era, as we read at the base of the pyramid.

Quadrangular de las monjas

67

El Mago

From there, we followed the route along the sacbe to the Quadrangle of the Birds and then that of the nuns(Nunnery Quadrangle), wherein, in each corner, there are covers like those used on Halloween day of a particular god called Chaac (the god of water). Here, I had to climb. Thank goodness that the stairs were made of aluminum, which made it easier for me to reach the quadrangle of the nuns, where you can see single-story buildings with sculptures of houses all the way. (It is so called because it is the name given to it by the Spaniards).

These quadrangles are unique; there is an echo, and all the structures are carved. We passed through one of the Mayan arches to go to the ball game. We used the wooden ramp to go down. Parts were under restoration and are closed to the public, but we managed to see the House of the Pigeons, the Great Pyramid, and the governor's palace. When I arrived at the palace, I was already exhausted. You must come early so that the sun does not dehydrate you.

(If you want to visit this UNESCO-recognized site, come early, and consider staying at least three hours.)

As it was lunchtime, we decided to go to Ticul. On the way, we pass through the colonial town of Santa Elena, where its church is on top of a pyramid. The Spaniards built the churches on top of the big pyramid to convince the Mayan that Christ was the only god to worship. So, they built most of the churches on top of the big pyramids. Ticul is an industrial town whose shoes are famous. It is remarkably close to Maní. After lunch, we went to see the church where Fray Diego de Landa hanged more than 2,000 Mayans because they did not want to convert to Christianity forcing to intimidate the rest of the population. He was responsible for destruction of idols and books and ironically, he is also the most significant source of information about Mayan culture. The church was built in 1562 and is dedicated to St. Michael the Archangel.

Maní

Nearby, there is a restaurant where they make typical Yucatecan food called Los Frailes, and in the hallway, one can observe how the Mayans wove *huipiles*. Those are cotton blouses that have little flowers and are worn by humans' ladies.

***

Day 4

The Next day we got up early., Ana told me: Lets explore the explore the hotel gardens." Oh, what a surprise! There were also pre-Hispanic constructions, a sacbe that went towards Uxmal, and remains of Mayan stone houses.

We continued along the road to Kabah. That city is also from the classic Puuc era and is on the way to Xpujil, this archeological site is from the preclassic to classic Mayan period that goes from 2000 BC to 250AD . The road practically divides the area into two archaeological zones. There have distinguished arches and Mayan masks.

Kabah

We continue along Road 261 towards Campeche. We observed the Puuc State Cultural Reserve and saw different birds, trees, and semi jungle forests. When we arrived in Hopelchén, we made a mistake; instead of taking the road on the right, we went to the left, so we could not see the pyramid of that city. Ana felt that we were lost and asked who was there. A gentleman explained that road 261 was very deserted, that we should continue through the reserve, in an hour, we would arrive at Xpujil.

We were happy and a little tired of seeing so many pyramids. For Ana, the road was a test drive. I could not sleep because it was poorly maintained and had huge potholes everywhere. It did not take an hour to get there; it took us three hours.

We begin to pass different hills and enter the biosphere of Calakmul. I let Ana know I had to pee, and suddenly, I smelled a big cat. At that, Roberto screamed, "Hurry up because there is an ocelot out there. Get in, everyone!" And we jumped into the car!

We followed the road and finally arrived at Xpujil.

Day 5

This city is in the state of Campeche halfway between the two capitals: Campeche and Chetumal. There, we had already set aside a hotel with its cabins. In the afternoon, we decided to visit the archaeological site of Xpujil.

Aninha gave up going to Becan because she was exhausted, and her boyfriend Leaf had the flu. So, we changed plans and went to rest.

There are more than six archaeological sites in this region, and they are from the classic Mayan period. It is estimated that Xpujil (meaning Cat's Tail) began in 400 BC and declined to AD 1100.

These cities are denser and less extensive than those in the east peninsula. Xpujil measures only twelve square kilometers, and the modern town of Xpujil is above this archaeological city. There, you can see more stelae and masks. In Xpujil, there are more than twenty-four buildings, and most are within a vast region of vegetation, which makes it more impressive.

(see Mayan route www.descubramexico.com)

It was like a new adventure, with strange smells everywhere. I hardly took my nose off the plants and the ground.

This area has lush vegetation, and so does the jungle. In that bleak place, the Mayans managed to live. The largest city is Calakmul, and they dominated the area and fought against Tikal and Palenque. We were going to visit Calakmul, but the tour guide warned us that the site was still very inappropriate to see and was only for ecotourism.

Day 6

Once we were all recovered, we decided to leave for Xul-ha. This village is south of Bacalar and is divided by the Los Rápidos River. The little hotel where we stayed was ideal for resting and recharging batteries for the return home. That day, we arrived at lunchtime. After lunch, we went to the lagoon to swim, enjoying the view as in Bacalar; you can also see different shades of blue.

Day 7

We left early so we could get to the airport. It was December 30, and the airport would indeed be packed. At about 12:30 p.m., we returned to Miami. We delivered the car, and at 6:00 p.m., I was already at home in my favorite armchair, where I meditated on everything I saw and thought:

"The Mayans respect nature, and even though they were always at war with each other (which I still don't understand), they care for their animals and plants."

I saw dogs in each small town, and a Mayan seller told us, "Free beings cannot be forced to change. We must let them be free because they will always reveal themselves. Here, the dogs are free. If they want to be with us, we give them food, shelter, medicine, and water. They come in the afternoon to the house. We open the gate, and they go wherever they like."

On this trip, I learned that you are better wherever you are as a family.

Respecting the opinions of others is essential to maintaining peace and tranquility, which is the sacbe to happiness.

Map Yucatán Mayan World

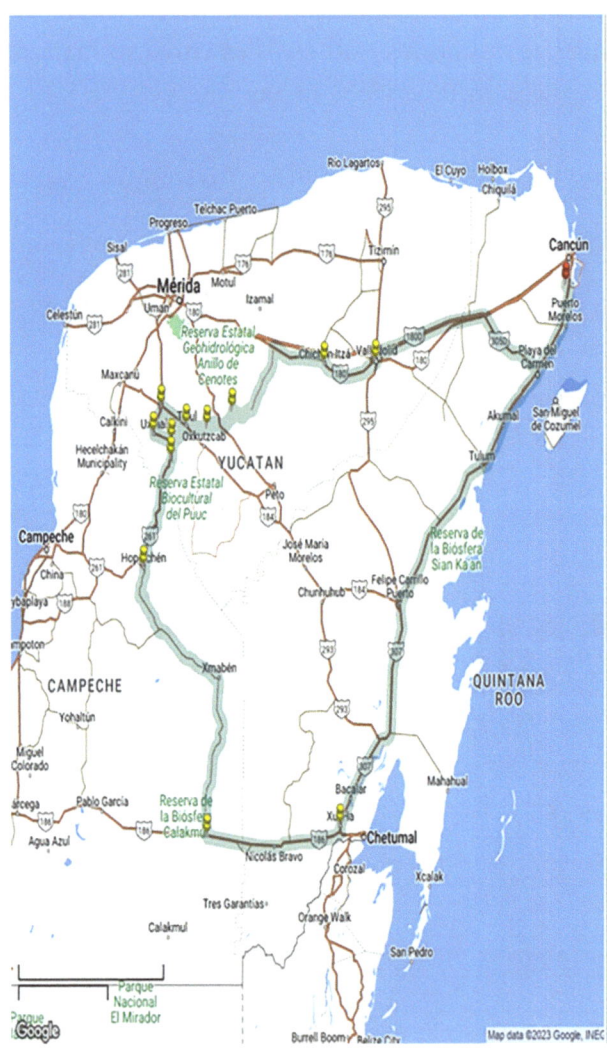

CONCLUSION:

"**M**itzi, what did you think of my trips?"

"I saw interesting places to observe how animals and plants adapt to each habitat. I learned how Native Americans and Mayans respect the forces of nature and how they learned to recycle and conserve water and food."

" The most important thing I can summarize is as follows:

Being with family and good friends makes life's path easier.

You must live every moment and enjoy it. The reality you see is yours alone and is the result of your thoughts because you interpret each one as you see it.

I must remember all the good things of the past and learn from my mistakes to guide me in the future because there is nothing to assume.

If you have doubts, clarify them. Assumptions lead us down the wrong path. Being (authentic) makes you trust yourself, and thus you will reach your goal.

Everything is possible; set your goals, love yourself, and continue. Have faith in yourself, for you can only reach the desired path with your will.

ACKNOWLEDGMENTS

Thanks

To God for giving me life

To my family, Ana, and Roberto

To my friend Bellini for teaching me to be a chill dog

To my friends, Nala, and Mitzi, for reminding me to be a dog.

To Abigail and Margaret, who helped me edit this book.

To Anita, Margaret, Roberto, and their children for accompanying me on my travels.

To my service dog trainer, Rose Lesniak

To Ana Pau who inspired me to write about my travels

To Liz, Vivian, Eva, and Volker for supporting me and encouraging me to draft this book.

TIPS AND RESOURCES

I t is essential to consider the following:

If you plan travel with a pet, it must be vaccinated and carry the medications required by its veterinarian and its rabies vaccination certificate and plaque, as it can be requested wherever it goes in the United States. In addition, the dog must be older than eight weeks.(www.akc.org)

To travel to Mexico, you must get a veterinary certificate approved by the Department of Agriculture of the United States of America (www.aphis.usda.gov).

It is good to check if the hotel or place you plan to stay accepts pets (www.bringfido.com).

In the United States, all La Quinta hotels accept pets.

The Following is a list of valuable references if you wish to travel to the visited areas.

National Parks www.nps.gov

Nevada www.travelnevada.com

Arizona www.visitarizona.com

Coloradowww.colorado.com

Utah www.utah.com

Wyoming[Visit Wyoming and Enjoy Your Wyoming Vacation (travelwyoming.com)](travelwyoming.com)

Cooperstown NY www.thisiscooperstown.com

Charleston www.Charlestonvisitorguide.com

 South Florida www.visitflorida.com

 In Mexico

Information about archaeological sites www.inah.gob.mx/zonas-arqueologicas

Mexicowww.visitmexico.com

Yucatan - Yucatan https://yucatan.gob.mx/

Campechehttps://Campeche Travel/

BIBLIOGRAPHY

Casas, Bartolomé de las, 1484-1566 - *Writtings of Bartolomé de las Casa* 1992 | English.

Díaz del Castillo, Bernal. - *Historia verdadera de la conquista de la Nueva España* - México: Editorial Porrúa, 1986.

Diego Landa -*Relación de las cosas de Yucatán*. Millwood, N.Y., Kraus Reprint Co., 1975.

Douglas, Marjory Stoneman. *The Everglades: River of Grass*. Sarasota, FL: Pineapple Press, 2007.

Mann, Charles *1491 New Revelations of the Americas before Columbus* Second Vintage Books Edition 2011.

McIver, Stuart B. *Glimpses of South Florida History* Florida Flair Books 1988.

Be a part and become a group member on Facebook Scotty Ways-los Relatos de Scotty.

www.ingramcontent.com/pod-product-compliance
Lightning Source LLC
Chambersburg PA
CBHW040847120626
46547CB00001B/60